A Thing With Teeth

AAIMA AZHAR

Copyright © 2023 Aaima Azhar
Cover design © Zainab Azhar

All rights reserved. No part of this book may be used or reproduced in any manner or capacity without written permission from the author except in the case of brief quotations embodied in critical articles and reviews.

To request permissions, contact the author at aaimaa.azhar@gmail.com

This is a work of fiction. Names, characters, places, and incidents are either the product of the author's imagination or are used fictitiously, and any resemblance to actual persons, living or dead, business establishments, events or locales is entirely coincidental.

Published by Aaima Azhar

A Thing With Teeth
ISBN: 978-1-7380195-0-2
Published in Canada

*the first page of the first book I write
will read an honest dedication,
not of the words or of the binding
or of the poetry –
but of myself and my every breath,
of my life and these hands,
of the things inside me,
of all that I am,
and all I ever have been,*

to You.

IV

Contents

Chapter I: Poetry That Hurts

Chapter II: The Bloody Drum

Chapter III: Prayers from the Stomach

| *A Thing With Teeth* |

Chapter I:
Poetry That Hurts

I have woven myself into these words for you.
bled across these pages for you.
I pray my soul reaches you well,
with love.

| *A Thing With Teeth* |

if it doesn't move you,
if it doesn't make sense to you,
if it doesn't leave you burning,
or healing, doesn't
leave your heart beating
faster than before –

it wasn't written, spoken, created
for you.

~ *and there is beauty in this*

I try to write from my head,
but it boils
from my chest, writhing and broken
like a raven
missing its wings, screaming
bloody murder
on my doorstep, *begging* me to end
the suffering I have caused
by trying to think
instead of feel.

| *A Thing With Teeth* |

keep your eyes off the knife your mother
keeps on her dressing table,
it's cold enough to wake her up
in the morning.

it's large enough to make your father stay.

it's sharp enough to cut
if you stare without asking
for permission,
even though you only
look because you like the way it
swallows all the light inside her room,
all the fear
inside of you.

she says, my dear,
this will be yours
one day.

we all crave romance,
want it carved across our throats in red
and blue,
want to have it
without begging for it –

although we beg all the same.

| *A Thing With Teeth* |

where is it?
I move my hands across my lips,
drop them to my shoulders. here?
I trace the collarbones, the hollow chest.
is it here?
I drag them to my belly, dig in, claw,
hold. here?

I reach inside, through the gut,
to the sobbing figure,
the contorted frame,
the charred, black, mass of me
that makes it hard to eat.

it's here.
I understand that it always has been,
I understand that
it might not ever leave. I understand that
it's going to hurt, but
everything that means something does.
the way you do, and my mother does.
the way my hands do when I write these things.
and when I braid my hair,

it hurts there too,
and when I cut it off,
it hurts there too.

I hope you're walking one day,
and it hits you –

the thought of me –

like a club to your chest, like
salt in a cut,
wraps its hands around your neck,
asks you what your name is now,
asks you why you left,
asks you how they are,
all those people
you pretended to be.

| *A Thing With Teeth* |

I have decided two things:

one, that grief is held between our bodies like a
tether, and this fraying rope keeps us alive,
draped over the precipice of the cliff,
the cruel marionettes dance,
whose puppeteer reads our heartache out like a book.

and the second is this:
that we forget is, perhaps,
the greatest mercy to mankind. that the ache
seeps in, then draws itself out,
then drips from our hearts,
and that we breathe again, and stumble back,
away from the gaping maw of the crater,
that we find scissors, cut the strings sewn
into our backs, wipe the blood from our spines,

and we run. and we run. and we run.
until the strings descend again.

two wolves are standing at your door, and you –
you are laughing;
you forgot to feed your mind last night.

| *A Thing With Teeth* |

and the soul can undo itself; we call this betrayal of
intuition, a form of treason against one's own heart,
the blunt knife in back,
the Antichrist to personal salvation.

we call this a lie, and it exists as an animal,
primal and in pain –

a thing with teeth.

I have a lot to say about you,
and all the ugly things I feel about you,
and the broken things that live inside you;
so I'll write about you,
and I'll write you into
this permanent story, this novel about you,
and I hope you like
how I make you immortal
through pen and paper,
I hope you like
how I make your dirty,
dark,
unholy,
twisted being
live forever.

| *A Thing With Teeth* |

when I was small
and longing didn't mean something,
didn't live in the hollow gutter of my neck,
in the carving knife cavern in my chest,
didn't tiptoe through my teeth,
make my lips hurt,
make each individual bone hurt,

when the doorbell rang and
someone always came home.
when waiting only happened on the playground
for some boy or another.

when it wasn't as alive as I am,
breathing me when I sleep –
if I ever do sleep –
shifting like this veil around me.

you were raised on concrete love,
had it poured into your breast,
and although it's hard to breathe,
you are proud of this.

you are only larger on the outside,
you never cry, you've forgotten how,
and you are proud of this.

~ but even the strongest man on earth
was given life
through a woman

| *A Thing With Teeth* |

the words inside me
are a bottomless well.

cut lesions across your heart and call it love.
ask the same question nine times before bed.
ask if it's supposed to wound like this.
ignore the answer,
because the blade was a gift.
tell yourself it's supposed to be difficult,
that the tenth answer doesn't exist.
tell yourself it's supposed to ache like this,
because the heart was a gift,
because the body should cave like this,
bare itself to the world like this,
inside out, upside down,
warm and alive like this.

| *A Thing With Teeth* |

I'm not sure if I *write* or if I unwind
myself on this paper for you, I'm not
sure if it relays the rage,
as the flame licking the insides of my mouth, but
I'm hoping that you feel it too, I'm hoping
that the spilled, the jilted parts of
my girlhood –
this unsatiated girlhood –
the bitter, left in the desert, left in
the grocery store overnight,
left to tie and untie, and tie and untie
the knots on her own,
the part that keeps the windows closed,
the part that still can't sleep alone,
is clear to you.

and I hope it hurts you too.

it feels alright to give in,
to strip the lips of English,
speak in this universal language, the
mother tongue of Grief.
to welcome, no,
to become the sadness,
the very colour blue – much less like the sky,
so much more like the Pacific –
and to drown in it.

| *A Thing With Teeth* |

on some days, you are a distant memory.
and on others,
the sickening lump in my stomach.

I'm angry and I'm allowed to be.

because back home doesn't exist.
it's just men who think between their legs.
it's just dirt.
it's just dirt,
like their wandering hands and filthy
rotten
politics.

it's pollution and it enters my heart,
coats the lining of my lungs,
so why do I still call myself
blood of your blood?
skin like yours? brown eyes like yours?

because I am half here, half there,
two kinds of soil inside my chest,

and I love this body.

God gave it to me.
and it does not belong to you.

~ it's not culture if it's violence
like an open wound
let it heal.

| *A Thing With Teeth* |

there is the half-love story,

and there is the empty notebook,

and the novel I never finished, the folded page,
the creases because I put the book down wrong.
every. single. time.
the stains and the anger in me.
anger at the book for being so tiring?
anger at the two, three, four minutes
I managed to keep my heart out of the pages,
my hands away from the cover,
the book from closing again, and again,
and again?
for pulling my hair out three chapters in?
for falling in love with every wrong character,
every wrong word, every. single. time?
for being too *tired* to read more than a line,
one paragraph, one page at a time?

and not the sleep tired, but the core tired.
the body. the bone. the soul tired.

~ *one of these days, I swear I'll read it all,*
I'll read it all the way through.

you're walking, and then you're running,
and then you're falling,
and your lips hit concrete,
your teeth rattle in their cage, your jaw cracks
and the blood runs, and you pull yourself up,
and you stumble, and your chest hits the pavement
again, and you crawl, and you walk, and you run,
and keep running, and

you're kissing the sidewalk again,
and you can't stop crying,
it doesn't hurt on your body,
it hurts inside – internal bruising, but the kind
in the back of the skull, the kind that feels like
screaming birds with the wings falling off,
with the beaks broken, the feet broken,
and you're getting up again, pulling rocks from your
hair, you're wiping spit off your face,
and the dirt, and the tears and you're laughing, and
you're sobbing, and
you're walking,
and you're running,
and –
…

| *A Thing With Teeth* |

the dead rot but so do the living,
and I would argue that the stench is worse
when they're six feet across from you,
but six feet under just the same,
alive by name but
crossed over to some distant shore,
only body left behind,
cruel anger left behind,
the deepest, ocean sadness
left behind.

and you, still under the same roof.
and you, still living with it.

the thing that wants to come out
doesn't always sound like rain, this time
it's ten different pitches of scream, this time
it's nails across a chalkboard, and I don't cover
my ears this time because I *need* to hear it
to remind myself that it exists,
to remind myself that if it's ugly
it's still valid, and if it's mangled
it's still real,

and if it tastes like tar, like feathers and tar,
like dust from a car
that ran my feet over, if it heals like
skin around glass,
it still exists.
like the brilliant sun, it still exists.
like every
human
inch of me,

it still exists.

| *A Thing With Teeth* |

we don't speak anymore.
not with our hearts.

there is a living fury
inside of you.
and you sound like thunder,
but the rain never follows,
and you know what love is,
but you're a fire-breathing thing;

but I know you're just as soft,
just as wanting,
and *afraid*,
as the rest of us.

| *A Thing With Teeth* |

last night, I dreamt about you.
I told you how you broke my heart,
showed you the aching organ
and the blood.
and I could tell this moment
apart from reality – because in this dream,
you understood.

they ask me to follow my gut,
but what if my own intuition
is a wounded animal,
and what if
I am more misguided than any
dirt
beat
soul you've ever known,
have you *seen* the way I cry
on my bedroom floor
when I can't stop thinking
what if, what if, what if

things had gone
differently?

~ this healing is not soft;
it is war, beneath my skin,
it is war

| *A Thing With Teeth* |

you tell me you don't like
the way I burn your toast.
you ask me if I'm surprised –
you never ate it anyway.

I tell you I don't like your smile.

you say
that's too far, and
I should calm down, where did
all of that come from?

I tell you,
I thought we were confessing,
and then,

I tell you I never loved you.

you put down your toast, and
I turn off the toaster.
I ask you if you're surprised;

you never speak to me again.

~ breakfast tastes better these days

when I cry,
I cry for you –
you are the knot in the back of my throat.

| *A Thing With Teeth* |

centerfold,
me on one page and you on the next,
the difference in the papers,
the crease in the middle,
the great divide,
the broken spine of the book,
the feeble string
holding it all together.

the things that can't hold us
together.
anymore.

I have learnt that he is a festering wound inside my chest. I have learnt that I can never stop loving him.

| *A Thing With Teeth* |

I want poetry that hurts, because in this
is a convoluted reflection of the state of our
half beating hearts, the type of declarations
that come from the stomach as hunger, the kinds that
live as the aches in our temples.

I would ask you to tell me one thing that lasted.
and you would list off the mundane. and I would ask
you to tell me one thing
that still feels like a current,
like the river in between the rocks,
like the water
that is alive and breathing, and splitting apart these
frail mountains.

tell me one thing
that makes it impossible for you to breathe.
I want poetry that hurts, and I want it driven, deep
knife between my ribs, burnt hair and burnt clothes,
and the red eyes that see so much more than this.

and an open chest.

with the heart on fire.

Chapter II:
The Bloody Drum

look at me like maybe I am poetry,
and I'll talk to you like
maybe you bring the rain.
I'll look at you like
maybe your heart is my heart.

~ *maybe you could share me with me*

| *A Thing With Teeth* |

"when you look into my eyes,
what do you see?"

"I see a forest. the kind with big old trees, and a clearing at the end, where the sunlight breaks in and drapes over everything."

"and when I smile?"

"the sun shines brighter."

"and when I cry?"

"a forest fire."

if it's just chemicals, then why do I bleed on the
inside when you're not here? why is there a hole
everywhere that you don't exist, in every breath you
don't draw in sync with mine, every step that isn't in
step with me, why is every void devoid of you only?
why do I want everything with you?

I'll tie the sun to your doorstep when you're cold
and I'll give you my sweater too, please just stay.

I know it's winter here sometimes but please, will
you stay? I know I can keep you warm.
I'll set myself alight if that's what it takes,
I'll *burn* if that's what it takes,
if it's just chemicals then why does it ache
when you come home a little bit late?

I want to dance in the kitchen with you.

I've been wanting to dance with you all day. the
music could be pots and pans and you can hold my
hand, and I just want to be a little girl with you. I'll
grow you a garden. I hate the feeling of dirt but I'll
rub it into every inch of my skin for you. I'll plant
tulips and daisies for you, please, tell me –

| *A Thing With Teeth* |

if this is chemical, then why did I know you before I knew you?
why have we lived this lifetime already?

why does it play in my heart over and over like a record, why does your voice do that thing that it does to me? why is it holy and soft, like molten glass, why does it break across my chest, *why* does it do this to me?

I love you. and if it's chemicals, I still love you. if I die today, I'll have loved the great chasm into a city covered in vines, the kinds you like, I'll have played, and played, and played like a child who never knew any better, and who was all the better for it. I'll have danced in every kitchen with you. and they'll bury me in your favourite dress. and I will love you even after that.

I try to write you –

your angel form and the soft hands,
the collar bones and the shoulder blades,
how they look like wings
and daggers all at once, the way I study,
and study, and study you.

but how can I write you? you are
the poem itself,
you are the story and the binding
and the book itself, and I read it,
and read it,
and read you.

| *A Thing With Teeth* |

provision is a deep act of worship,
not of the material, but of the intangible mixed
with the mundane, the cup of tea, the gentle
awakening,
the tucking in, the taking out, the smile
that belongs to them.
the smiling often.
the *existing* for the one that you love,
your body, your heart, entirely at their service.
the loving with deep sincerity.
taking every breath for them, and them only.
making sure that if there is anyone they know
who knows them like a child,
like the back of their hand,
like a sacred ritual, like a morning prayer,
it's you.

you say things without saying them.
you are a foreign part
of this familiar body,
and you own the skin,
and everything within,
and you cross every border –
every country is named after you.
you touch like brushstroke
on barren canvas,
and the canvas belongs to you.

you paint it like da Vinci;
I become your Mona Lisa,
your masterpiece, your muse.

and I have loved before,

but not on fire –

not like this.

if the grave will have you before it has me,
I pray it holds you with the arms of a mother.
that the dirt is soft, that the dark is kind,
and with every visit,
I bring you my warmth,
and that you feel it as you lie before me,
in the Earth's embrace, instead of mine,
wrapped in white,
instead of me.

as you drift like water
from me, like a wave,
as I am left here, like Ali
over Fatima's grave,
as I speak to you in poetry, just as he did,
as you respond in my heart
just as she did.

I pray the love is buried with you,
as you are called from this world.
I pray to join you soon after,
as a gift from our Lord.

I want to be taken care of, like a flower.

watered and soft,
spoken gently to,

always in the sun, always next to you.

| *A Thing With Teeth* |

I will have you,
with your crooked smile,
and the funny way you laugh, or else
I will not have you.

I will have you,
with your convoluted past,
and your heart wide open, or else
I will not have you.

I will have you in ways
you have not had yourself, I will
have you in ways that will
bring you to your knees, drag you
closer to God, make you
cry, and *pray*, and *cry*, I will
have you in ways
that will devastate your reality,
tear it apart just to build it up again, and
disturb your peace,
intrude upon your soul,
or else
I will not have you.

~ *I am not for the weak at heart*

you move like
the season of the rains, you came
out of nowhere, you walk
like a body of water –

the whole world is pleading:
just one drink.

| *A Thing With Teeth* |

if you looked like them
there would be no you,
and in this is a tragedy, a sort of
loss I cannot describe to you –
the idea of you,
missing from yourself,
from this place that is riddled with differences,
no two flowers just the same,
in this springtime, this
garden beauty of it all.

~ you are love in human form, and
I adore you.

there stood the moon,
and his half-lit face,
glowing in a way
only he knows how to.

and there stood you, all of yourself,
not a single piece missing,
not a hair, not a nail left untouched
by the sun –

the easiest decision I've ever made.

| *A Thing With Teeth* |

the parts of you that sound sad,
that draw blood,
that hurt to say,
that are hard to hold –

let me hold them with you.

and I know it'll get all over you,
stain your shirt and maybe your skin.

and that's okay too, I'll just sit here,
I'll just wash it out with you.

or you can have mine, you can
have it all, you can
maybe
have me, too.

I was imagining us five or so years into the future. we're still young, but you, loving your grey hairs and your collared shirts and ties, practically asking for your thirties to begin. me, in your sweater, basically drowning in it, your coffee cup in my hand but, of course, it's filled with tea.

and the sun. yes, the sun, the morning ray seeping in. the curtains are white, flowy, the way I like. the couches are anything but black. anything but white. the kitchen is every pretty photograph we used to send each other, meshed into one. it's simple, old fashioned, like us. full of plants. flowers in the sink. and we're having breakfast, but before breakfast we talk. or don't talk. we just stare.

and you're as beautiful as the day I first saw you.
just as painfully beautiful.
heartbreakingly beautiful.

I kept imagining and I dreamt up a cat, asleep on the windowsill. I imagined pancakes. I imagined your laugh, the way it rings around the room. perhaps a bit deeper now, a bit older. just as soft. I imagined our house, small, cottage-like. I imagine you designed it. or maybe you didn't, and it's perfect either way.

| *A Thing With Teeth* |

I tried to imagine a country, but the truth is, you are my flag and my border. everything is trivial but you, and the truth is, I'm still stuck on you. it's a simple thing,

I'm still stuck on you. I imagined your gentle laugh lines, your knowing eyes, the bridge of your nose, the angle of your lips, the tilt of your head. the way you still make my stomach turn.

I imagined the love, like a tether between us, connecting our middles, the pull and the sheer impossibility of trying to fight it. the knowing we never would.

the correctness, the rightness of you. I imagined watching you eat. drinking from the spot on the glass that I drank from. watching you dress. packing you lunch. leaving you with a kiss at the door.

I imagined the warmth, then. even in your parting.
but this time, knowing,
you'll come back home.

you're shaped like love, I feel
God when I see you, I see
myself when I see you,
I hear this song I used to listen to, I hear
birds – not just the singing but the wings,
every beat that carries flight – you must
believe me when I tell you, that
I hear this when I look at you.

you laugh and it moves me to tears.
how vicious, how disgraceful
any heart has been in mishandling yours.
and this sky, this earth, and our Creator
is my witness to how I love you,
how softly.
I will love you.

| *A Thing With Teeth* |

if I could take a dagger to your hurting,
cut it from your body,
I would be hilt deep in your flesh,
in an instant.

replace it with green and me, and
three fresh flowers. one for every beat my
heart skips, in the time it takes you
to get from the garden to my door,
from the front door to me,
in the time it takes you to pour my tea,
in the spaces you cry, and
you ask me why
I love you like this,
you ask me how
I found you like this,

but if *anyone*
deserves, I mean truly
deserves,

it's you. it's you. it's you.

you laugh so easily.

like falling glass, or
mountain water –

both crystal clear, and
somewhat dangerous,

the way
they cut across the skin.

| *A Thing With Teeth* |

you live within me,
I have you
branded on my mouth in red,
written in the corners of my lips,
in the spaces between my ribs, you are

my tribe,
my temple,
my desert shade,

the way you
own these lungs, and this
bloody drum, the way it
beats for you.

how are you water and fire, all at once?
how are you waterfall, waves crashing shore,
fountain glinting in the sun, but also that sun
yourself? how do I burn like this? when you smile
like that? why do I ache like this? like I see you, and
my eyes drink, and drink, and drink but my skin still
blisters from the heat. like it's never enough. like I
always want more. because you belong with me, in
one body, one soul, one heart beating, drum beating,
until the city hears it, until the Earth sings along.

how do you mend me like this? like a prayer?
like everything gentle in one place. like crying in my
mother's arms, like laughing with my brother when
everything hurts, like being held
when my tendons resist my bones,
when I bleed in places I shouldn't, how
do you put me back together like this?

and, God, how do you love me
like every storm that has ever made love
to the sky, made the oceans turn over,
made the mountains say their name, made prayer the
only grace? made those very prayers come true.
made poetry out of the mess.
and loved the mess too.

| *A Thing With Teeth* |

I hope to see you again,
in the world after this, when there is
less of this place,
crowding the space
between our hearts, I hope
you look for me then, I think

you are a mecca for love,
you were made out of love.
and I was made to love you,
and for you, I speak in tongues
that only recognize your name,
and when I pray,
I beg Allah,
to *please* take care of you.

*~ this lion behind my ribs,
he weeps for you*

I have nothing to say, but that I miss you.
that every piece of me does.
that I am deeply unwound without you.
that time is not fair to me without you.
that I am a nighttime grove, with weeping trees,
tired leaves, no fireflies and no butterflies
without you.

the romantic telephone:
the commitment to sitting down,
spending sixty seconds on the dial,
the slow turns and the soft clicks,
and the soft way you answer it.
how my stomach turns, how the wire turns
in my hands, and how my hands shake.
how your voice doesn't –
slipping roses
through the receiver,
bedtime stories
keeping me up.

~ *"hello, you*
I've missed your sound."

"hello, back. I've missed yours too."

he smells like pine and river,
mixed with foreign flowers,
and the wind they belong to.

he reminds me of skipping rocks,
and the highway stops,
and the corner shops,
and every train I watched,
ran after,
caught up to,
like vagabond, like nomad,

like mountain rain,

and the ferocious way it pours.

how gut wrenching,
how terrifying,
to be this choked up
in love, this
decapitating affair of
a basal, bleating
heart, how
foolish, how
tiring, to be this
neck deep,
in love, to be this
throat sore, this
head spinning, this
soul aching,
in love.

and if you smile like that again,
I'll rip these clouds from their mount,
I'll bring you every last one,
I'll leave them on your doorstep, and
I'll bring the rain too.
I'll bring myself too.

| *A Thing With Teeth* |

I am writing to remind you
of the place you hold within me.
I am writing to touch your heart
until my hands can touch you.
I am writing to make you smile –
that smile that drips in honey,
that makes my skin feel warmer and
my breaths come shorter.
I want you to know that this is how I love you.

I love you like I can't breathe.
and I can't breathe without you.
I love you like my heart sees you,
I love you like you are the softest thing.
I love you in your day
and even more in your night.
in your rain. in your grace.
this is how I love you.

Chapter III:
Prayers From the Stomach

if there is a drought, then ask it *why?*
does it adore the dunes?
does it find the sand beautiful?
is it beloved to the flower that grows there,
and there only?
does it weep when it is washed away?
and if the rain is not welcome here,
then honour that.
if this desert gives you life, then honour that.

A Thing With Teeth

and when we can no longer stand the grief,
we stand for each other,
cupped hand under cheek,
forehead to creased forehead,
chest to hurting, burning chest –

and we sing.
we sing the wound into callous,
the callous into scar,
scar into flower wreaths around our heads,
never asking "why" only "how
can I help you through your red
into your softest shade of green, how
can I soothe the part that aches, how
can I love and love and *love* you?"

I want to emphasize that I am more than this.
because most of the tree is underground, and most of
the ice is under the water, and most of me is under
my skin, growing inwards and upwards, in every
direction that I pray, every moment that my voice
tumbles from my tongue, that my tears wet this mat,
that my heart breaks and my God tells me
"I am near [2:186]"

in every soft breath He breathes into me, in every
stomach-ache that brings me one inch closer
to my Home, in every night I don't sleep.
I only cry.
I only hope.
I only ask that my Lord reaches past His skies and
the void inside me, that He unfolds the creases in the
corners of my lungs, that He widens the alleys in
these animal veins,
that I am guided,
that I am given even one word of assurance –

but the word never comes.

the love comes instead,
and it consumes me,
it becomes me, I *am* love, I refuse not *be* love,
I refuse not to smother every heart
in ferocious love. I will paint it across my face until I
am *dripping* in love –

because my Lord teaches me this:

"to love is difficult [2:216]"

but I will tear myself apart just to know Divinity,
until I am born, and reborn,
and He has forgiven my every downfall,
and He has spoken through me, until
I live for His love, until I emanate His decree,
until every soul that passes mine sees my roots
running miles deep, running mountains deep,
running oceans below my feet,

growing flowers out of my ribs in all the directions
that I call out to Allah,
and despite the blood I only say

"please come here, please pick a few,
they were grown through this clay for you,
and you,
and you."

the only thing I've ever wanted
is to not want anything anymore,
to be so whole on the inside,
that when I am cut
navel to neck, when I am
entirely inverted,
where my entrails fall out –
I only smile, and I laugh.
I only bend down, pick them back up,
put them back inside, wash the red off, and
walk home, and go up to Your room,
tell you You're enough, You have always
been enough, been more
than enough
for me.

| *A Thing With Teeth* |

if you are looking for something soft
and easy:
you are in the wrong part of understanding
this woven concept of yourself –
didn't your body beg you to honour
its inability to be smooth, to be milk
and glass, didn't it tell you
my name is not a petal, it is a weed in the field
of this vastness that is your existence,
the kind that fruits need to survive,
the kind where flowers are born and die in their
efforts to replicate even one leaf?

if you are looking for gentle,
rolling hills and a smile that curves
instead of falling over the side of your face,

break your mirror.
because it won't do anything for you,
because you and your feral beauty
do not exist in a reflection or a sketchbook page;
you exist in the dirt and the rocks,
and the smell of earth
in a rain flooded orchard,
and in every garden.

some days

you are going to feel it all over again,
and it will be difficult for a moment,
and you will remember it all,
and your chest will burn,
and your heart will thrum,
like a bulb burning out,

and it will *hurt* –

let it.

| *A Thing With Teeth* |

the prayers that come from the pit of your stomach
are poetry.

dear Angel of Death,

when you come, I pray you find me
covered in light and doves,
and all the good I have done.

dear Angel,
if this world, like a coin in your hand,
fits neatly between your feet,
who am *I* to ask for more time?
for a moment more inside of it?

dear Angel,
please be gentle,
when you drag from my mouth and eyes,
this soul, from this mortal body,
that has prayed and sinned,
has loved and lied.

dear Angel,
take me with you,
when I am beautiful on the inside,
to my grave
when I am walking kindness,
to return me to my Lord.

~ Dear Azra'il

| *A Thing With Teeth* |

hold it there, the newness, let it sit
between your teeth. don't speak,
don't try to weave it into "what it should be,"
just
let the breath come and let the breath go.

let the year dribble out,
ink spilling from your lips,
the way it *wants* to spill, let it stain your clothes,
let it write itself, be born and reborn
from your open mouth, let the good exist,
let the bad stay too, keep it under your tongue.
keep the love there too.
let the honey melt there,
and let the bees live too.

does the heart not pray?
each thump, a quiet ask, the push and shove
of every valve,
the rush of blood, pilgrims at a gate,
the steady chant, bend, and bow –

tell me, now, does the heart not pray?

it says to me,
"ask your Lord what He breathed into you,
ask Him how He gave you me, ask him how
you began as clay, and now you *walk,*
and *talk,*
and *breathe*, please

ask Him how He keeps you alive,
how He grants you this love,
allows you this grief,
forgives your resentment,
when you fall to your knees,
when you search for light,
and forget about me."

| *A Thing With Teeth* |

the same way the tide turns,
I am moved to say this to you:

it has been you, yourself,
within the confines of this
human vessel, it has been *you*
who is so much, who is transcendent
of the blood beneath you.
it has been you all along.
you are the love and the light,
gently molded by Divinity, you
who was created, not to traverse life,
but to conquer it, to cultivate and unhinge it —
to live, rather than exist.
you are not this frame, this given form —

you are the home existing within it.

we were made
to build and rebuild,
and to love and lose,
and grieve,
and forget,

and to love again.

~ you will move
and your heart will move with you.

if the stars make pilgrimage too,
what gives us the right
to do anything but walk,
endless circles around Your home,
to run from peak to peak,
on legs we do not deserve,
to touch that holy stone –
a sea of black and white
with every kind of sadness,
every piece of joy,
laid open and unveiled,
bare feet, and bare bones
before You?

I will take flight.
and the wind will whip my hair,
and I will find it hard to breathe,
and I will see the city beneath my feet,
and I may touch the ground once or twice,
but I refuse,
I refuse
not to fly.

| *A Thing With Teeth* |

some days, I am Elven,
I am Dragonic, I speak
Fairy and walk with a prince.

and some nights, I am human,
so painfully mortal,
and I bleed when I am cut –
and I am cut often –
but I stand on my own feet,
and the flesh is still intact,
and I have a heart that beats,
and I have a heart that loves.

~ so tell me,
isn't this magic?

this feels like I've known you from before,
when our souls were gathered together,
and we knew our purpose,
the promise we made, and
the Entity we serve,
and how we are all in this together.

I remember you from then.
my essence remembers how you feel,
how you look on the inside,
how you cry, how you smile,
how you
cave in on yourself,
and how you bloom,
and bloom,
and bloom.

and you are *still* just as kind,
still just as beautiful.

~ *I think your rūh knows mine,
I hope I see you in the afterlife.*

A Thing With Teeth

in my heart,
I grow flowers in my garden, and
they stay alive.
in my heart,
my mother lives forever.
in my heart, I give more than I take,
I spend only on things that
change the world.

in my heart,
those who left us too soon
are still here with us.

in my heart,
you are still here with me.
in my heart, you never leave.

in my heart,
I forgive the hand I am dealt,
I forgive you, and I forgive them,
and I learn
to forgive myself.

do you not see yourself?
for the ocean you are?
a walking testament to all that is wild,
all that is free, and open, and wise –

everything that is present,
yet far away, all at once.

you are a wave,
a tsunami,
a reckoning current.

even the moon cannot tame you.

| *A Thing With Teeth* |

tonight, I spoke to the rain,
and her winds carried my words up to Allah.
of this, my heart is certain.

He will answer my prayers
as gently as this water
loves the earth back to life –
of this, my rūh is absolutely certain.

and her laughter was a lullaby,
her smile told me this: "it does not matter,
if the world is not as soft as you are,
is not as gentle –
because here, you are enough, and here,
you are home, and here,
you are the love they never gave you.
the love they ate alive."

~ dear mama,
 I would tear the sky apart for you, and still,
it could never be enough.

| *A Thing With Teeth* |

you don't say much,
but you love me quietly,
whether you're bringing me more mangoes
than I could eat in a week,
or you're fixing up my room
without me asking you to,
or the way you ask me "how was school?"
when you mean "how is your heart,
my dearest daughter, how are you?"

I'm good Baba, I'm here because of you,
your strength and the difficult work you do,
and the home you left all too soon.
Baba, I've made it this far because of you.

I know you say it in the way
that you care for me,
but this is how I'll say it to you:

dear Baba, thank you,
and I really love you.

I want to be so soft that every word I have to say
is coated in love, is so entirely
made up of love, I want to heal
and never hurt.
I want to be so intensely, so fervently,
so incessantly *there* for myself,
and for all the hearts
that my heart touches.
tell me,
why else was I placed here?

why else?

if not to love to death?
if not to love for my life?

| *A Thing With Teeth* |

sometimes,
the pain of this world is overwhelming.
and it tires me. and I get sad. so hauntingly sad.
I want to tear it off the face of this Earth.
cleanse her, to the core,
to the bones, if she has any.
then ask her to start all over again.

but I know I'm just one girl.
and the suffering of this world is large –
(and it tires me, and I get blue) –
but never larger than love.
never larger than faith.
and all this *life* we must go on living.

someone breaks my window,
makes a home out of my house,
and I walk out the front door.
I don't return.

the next day, I live like a bird,
somewhere between God and the trees,

and the Moon knows me better than
I know myself now,
I forget the rest, but
I live with her now,

she teaches me things, and
I know how to love now.

Acknowledgments

I'll begin by saying these words were written by me through inspiration from the beautiful souls surrounding me, and the ever-present inspiration of Divinity.

Thank you to my lovely sister, a piece of my heart, for editing this and encouraging me to put this collection out into the world. I genuinely could not have done this without you. And my parents for loving me through every stage reflected herein. And to my brother, for simply being a brother.

And thank you to my soulmate, my whole world, my Mohamed, for being a constant in this everchanging landscape of creating art. So many of these poems are for you – but I think you knew that.

Finally, thank you to all my readers and supporters, including those from my early days of writing and sharing poetry. It is your love, reflections, and motivating messages that have helped me bring this book into fruition. I pray it moves you, just as all of you have moved me. Ameen.

www.ingramcontent.com/pod-product-compliance
Lightning Source LLC
Chambersburg PA
CBHW021128080526
44587CB00012B/1186